Published by Bore No More!™
877-457-3981
Bore No More is a registered trademark

Printed in the USA

Book design by Ivana Brajković
Photography by Mark Williams Photography

This book and additional 7 of hearts cards may be ordered directly from the publisher. Please contact Bore No More at www.BoreNoMore.com.

ISBN: 978-0-692-27259-6

SIGNIFICANCE...

IN SIMPLE MOMENTS

BY JON PETZ

To Nathan's family. . .

May a 7 of Hearts one day be passed to you,
or may this book end up in your hands, wherever you may be.

TABLE OF CONTENTS

"THEY REALLY WANTED
DAVID
COPPERFIELD..."

IT'S
SHOWTIME!

As I crossed the threshold onto the stage that day, my stomach had the requisite butterflies that always happened before a show. I had my props; I was locked, loaded, and ready.

But this was not a big show. There was no crowd of adoring fans. There were no spotlights. There wasn't even really a stage.

This was not what I had been dreaming of.

This was not Vegas.

This was a hospital room.

I didn't even really want to be there. But I took a breath, stepped into that room, put on a smile, and told myself, "It's Show Time!" I had no idea that this performance would become the most memorable show of my life.

My friend Linda volunteers for a charity that helps children and their families who are battling life threatening illness. She asked me to do a little magic show for a sick boy at the local hospital.

As a newly self-employed magician trying to make my way in showbiz, I didn't view this hospital "gig" as ideal for two reasons:

I WAS DREAMING OF

LAS VEGAS

and I didn't like **HOSPITALS**

LINDA SAID THIS BOY WAS A HUGE FAN OF MAGIC, HE WASN'T DOING VERY WELL, AND SHE HOPED A FEW SLEIGHT OF HANDS TRICKS WOULD BOOST HIS SPIRITS.

MAGIC HAD ALWAYS DONE THAT FOR ME. MY FATHER HAD WOWED ME WITH A SIMPLE PENNY TRICK WHEN I WAS SEVEN YEARS OLD AND I WAS INSTANTLY HOOKED. MAGIC BECAME MY LOVE, MY DELIGHT, AND MY PASSION.

I CONTINUALLY WORKED ON MY SKILLS AND MADE CASH AS A TEENAGER DOING BIRTHDAY PARTY SHOWS FOR KIDS. I PERFORMED THROUGHOUT COLLEGE AND EVEN AS I ENTERED THE PROFESSIONAL WORKING WORLD. AT AGE 25, I MADE MY FIRST ATTEMPT AT LEAVING MY "REAL JOB" TO PERFORM MAGIC FULL TIME.

THE CALL FROM LINDA CAME DURING THIS TIME FRAME.

"WELL... UHH, I'M PRETTY BUSY..." I STAMMERED, FEELING UNCOMFORTABLE WITH THE SITUATION.

LINDA KEPT TALKING, "I KNOW, JON, AND THAT'S GREAT, BUT THIS BOY NATHAN REALLY WANTS TO MEET DAVID COPPERFIELD, AND WE DON'T THINK THAT IS GOING TO BE ABLE TO HAPPEN. SO... I'M ASKING YOU."

"WHAT!?" I SHRIEKED. "DAVID COPPERFIELD?!"

MY MIND WENT INTO HYPERDRIVE AND STARTED CHURNING UP EXCUSES.

Copperfield!? How can I possibly compare to David Copperfield?!

I'm **JUST** a magician in Columbus, Ohio.

I'm **JUST** a no-name performer - not a headliner celebrity with his own Las Vegas show.

He's a star - I'm **JUST** Jon Petz!

What could I possibly do that would compare to one of the world's greatest magicians?

I'M NOT SURE WHAT CAME OUT OF MY MOUTH, BUT ALL I HEARD WAS LINDA SAYING, "THANK YOU, JON! NATHAN WILL BE SO HAPPY. CAN YOU COME TODAY?"

"TODAY?! WELL, I . . . I . . . I GUESS SO."

I PACKED MY POCKETS WITH STANDARD MAGIC STUFF AND OFF I WENT.

ARRIVING AT THE ONCOLOGY WARD, I FELT MY ANXIETY RISE AND BUTTERFLIES TAKE FLIGHT IN MY STOMACH AS I SOON ENTERED NINE-YEAR-OLD NATHAN'S ROOM.

HIS MOTHER, FATHER AND SISTER WERE PERCHED ON A SMALL COUCH AGAINST THE WALL. STANDING NEXT TO THEM WAS A PRIEST.

ALREADY UNEASY AND QUEASY, THE SICK FEELING IN MY STOMACH NOW FLOWED THROUGHOUT MY ENTIRE BODY AS I GREETED THEM.

I TURNED AND SAW THE HOSPITAL BED ON THE OTHER SIDE OF THE ROOM. A SMALL BOY, NEARLY HIDDEN BY ALL THE MACHINES CONNECTED TO HIS FAILING BODY, LOOKED UP AT ME.

EVEN THOUGH I KNEW IT WAS INAPPROPRIATE, I STOOD AND STARED, TOTALLY AT A LOSS FOR WORDS.

NATHAN STARED BACK AT ME WITH CAUTIOUS EYES OF WONDER—NOT EXCITED WONDER, BUT THE PUZZLED KIND. HE DIDN'T KNOW WHO I WAS OR WHY I WAS THERE. THIS AWKWARD MOMENT ONLY FURTHERED MY UNEASINESS. I WANTED TO SAY, "HI, I KNOW YOU WANTED DAVID COPPERFIELD, BUT SORRY, KID, ALL YOU GET IS . . .

JUST ME."

FINALLY, THE SILENCE WAS BROKEN WHEN HIS MOTHER STOOD AND SAID, "NATHAN, THIS IS JON, AND HE'S A MAGICIAN."

AND A TRUE MAGICAL THING HAPPENED. SUDDENLY THOSE EYES OF CAUTIOUS WONDER CHANGED TO EAGERNESS AND EXCITEMENT. THE SOLEMN MOOD IN THE ROOM SHIFTED A LITTLE BIT.

NATHAN SAT UP IN HIS BED AS BEST HE COULD AS I PUT OUT MY HAND TO GREET HIM. AS HE SHOOK MY HAND, I HEARD A LOUD BREATHING SOUND. HE WASN'T ABLE TO SPEAK BECAUSE OF THE MASK AND EQUIPMENT HOOKED INTO HIS RESPIRATORY SYSTEM. IT WAS BREATHING FOR HIM.

NATHAN'S WARM HANDSHAKE STARTED TO SETTLE MY DISCOMFORT, AND I NERVOUSLY LAUNCHED INTO "SHOW" MODE. I PULLED OUT A TRICK I'D BEEN DOING FOR TEN YEARS INVOLVING LITTLE SPONGE BALLS.

I STOOD BY THE SIDE OF NATHAN'S BED AND PLACED ONE BALL INTO MY HAND, THEN HANDED HIM THE OTHER BALL. NATHAN'S EYES FIXATED ON MY CLOSED FIST. I OPENED MY HAND SLOWLY. NO BALL! (NOPE, NOT UP MY SLEEVES; I HAD NONE!) NATHAN'S EYES QUICKLY DARTED BACK TO MINE WITH A MYSTIFIED "WHAT?!" LOOK.

"NATHAN, WHY DON'T YOU CHECK YOUR HAND?" I SUGGESTED.

HE OPENED HIS HAND. MAGICALLY THERE APPEARED TWO BALLS, THE BALL HE WAS HOLDING AND THE BALL I HAD JUST "VANISHED."

HE LOOKED AT ME WIDE-EYED AND FULL OF ENERGY, HIS EAGER GLEAM OF EXCITEMENT SAYING, "**DO IT AGAIN.**"

THE TALK BEHIND ME IN THE ROOM SUBSIDED. NATHAN'S SISTER PEERED INTO WHAT WE WERE DOING. NATHAN AND I DID THE TRICK AGAIN . . . AND AGAIN . . . WITH THREE BALLS, THEN FOUR. BEFORE LONG, LITTLE RED SPONGE BALLS WERE OVERFLOWING FROM NATHAN'S HAND.

EACH TIME HE SAW ONE, HIS EYES GRINNED AT ME TWINKLING WITH AWE. THE BREATHING RESPIRATOR KICKED INTO A HIGHER GEAR AS HIS EXCITEMENT GREW. AND MY AUDIENCE GREW TOO. ALL FIVE PEOPLE IN THE ROOM WERE TRANSFIXED.

IT WAS A TRUE "SHOWTIME" MOMENT, ONE OF THOSE TIMES WHEN YOU NEVER KNEW YOU WOULD BE IN THE SPOTLIGHT, BUT SUDDENLY YOU ARE AND YOU HAVE TO BE AT YOUR BEST.

WITH THIS EXCITEMENT CAME AN INCREASING COMFORT LEVEL WITHIN ME AS I THOUGHT, "THIS IS SHOWTIME! I CAN DO THIS."

NEXT, I PULLED A DECK OF CARDS FROM MY POCKET. "THIS IS A UNIQUE CARD TRICK, AND I NEED TO BORROW A CREDIT CARD," I PROCLAIMED.

THE PRIEST OFFERED UP HIS CARD. (REALLY!) JUST IN CASE SOMETHING WENT AMISS, I ALSO PULLED OUT MY OWN CREDIT CARD. MINE HAS MY PICTURE ON IT, ONE OF THOSE SECURITY PHOTOS TO PROTECT ME IN CASE SOMEONE WOULD TRY TO "BORROW" MY CARD. I SET BOTH CREDIT CARDS ASIDE.

THEN, AS NORMALLY HAPPENS IN CARD TRICKS, SOMEONE NEEDED TO SELECT A CARD, SO I ASKED THE PRIEST TO DO IT.

HE PICKED A CARD AND THEN RETURNED IT TO THE DECK. SHORTLY AFTER HIS SELECTED CARD WAS RETURNED TO THE DECK, IT TURNED BLANK. THAT'S RIGHT. THE FACE OF THE CARD THE PRIEST HAD JUST HELD BECAME FULLY WHITE, THE IMAGE COMPLETELY GONE.

I PLAYED THE "PANICKED MAGICIAN IN TROUBLE" ROLE AND SUGGESTED NATHAN USE MY CREDIT CARD TO PURCHASE A NEW PACK OF CARDS. BUT WHEN HE PICKED UP MY CREDIT CARD, MY SMALL PHOTO ON IT WAS NOW GONE—ERASED FROM THE PLASTIC OF MY CREDIT CARD.

THINGS WERE

DISAPPEARING!

In a state of alarm,
I suggested we then use the priest's credit card.
Nathan picked up the priest's card.

"TURN IT
OVER!"

I said.

STUCK NOW ON THE CREDIT CARD – YUP, ON THE BACK OF THE PRIEST'S CARD – WAS A MINIATURE PHOTO. IT WAS A PHOTO OF ME, SMIRKING AND POINTING AT A PLAYING CARD. THE SAME CARD THE PRIEST HAD SELECTED AND THE ONE THAT HAD ERASED ITSELF.

THE ROOM ERUPTED IN HOWLS OF ASTONISHMENT. THEY PASSED AROUND THE CREDIT CARD FOR ALL TO SEE. AND NATHAN'S EYES? YOU SHOULD HAVE SEEN THEM GLOW!

NOW WE REALLY HAD A SHOW GOING ON!

I HAD ONE MORE CLASSIC TRICK TO SHARE WITH THEM AND I WANTED NATHAN TO TRULY EXPERIENCE THE MAGIC ON THIS ONE. THERE'S A BIG DIFFERENCE BETWEEN WATCHING A MAGIC TRICK AND TRULY BEING A PART OF ONE.

I ASKED NATHAN TO TAKE ANY CARD FROM THE DECK.

HE SELECTED THE 7 OF HEARTS.

I HAD HIM *sign* IT AS HIS SIGNATURE WOULD CONFIRM THIS WAS THE CARD HE SELECTED. THERE ISN'T ANOTHER 7 OF HEARTS IN THE WORLD THAT WOULD LOOK LIKE THIS ONE HE HAD WRITTEN ON.

I PLACED NATHAN'S CARD FACE DOWN INTO THE MIDDLE OF THE DECK, LOSING IT FOR THE MOMENT. I HAD NATHAN TURN UP THE TOP CARD TO SHOW IT WAS NOT HIS SIGNED 7 OF HEARTS. THEN I ASKED HIM TO DO A LITTLE MAGIC OF HIS OWN AND TAP THE TOP OF THE DECK AND TURN OVER THE TOP CARD AGAIN. HE DID. AND SOMEHOW, THE TOP CARD HAD MAGICALLY CHANGED INTO 7 OF HEARTS. YES, NATHAN'S 7 OF HEARTS WITH NATHAN'S SIGNATURE.

THE YOUNG BOY LOOKED UP AT ME CONFUSED. SO DID EVERYONE ELSE. HOW COULD THAT BE? SO WE DID THE TRICK AGAIN, PUTTING

THE 7 OF HEARTS DEEPER INTO THE DECK AND AGAIN CHECKING TO MAKE SURE THE TOP CARD WASN'T HIS. THE ARTIFICIAL BREATHING MACHINE TOOK A DEEP BREATH, AND NATHAN TAPPED THE TOP CARD, AND TURNED IT OVER. YUP, AGAIN, IT WAS HIS SIGNED 7 OF HEARTS!

NATHAN COULDN'T GET ENOUGH OF THIS FUN. HE GIGGLED WITH HIS WIDE AND INSPIRING EYES AND HIS FAMILY LAUGHED ALONG WITH HIM.

I PUT THE 7 OF HEARTS UNDER HIS WATER CUP, IN HIS HAND, IN THE DECK. EVERY TIME, HE USED HIS NEWLY LEARNED POWERS TO DO HIS LITTLE MAGIC. AND EVERY TIME HE TOUCHED THE TOP OF THE DECK AND TURNED IT OVER, THERE IT WAS—NATHAN'S 7 OF HEARTS WITH HIS NAME WRITTEN ON IT.

FOR THE SHOW'S FINALE, I THREW THE ENTIRE DECK OF CARDS UP TO THE CEILING OVER NATHAN'S BED AND ALL THE CARDS CAME TUMBLING DOWN.

ALL EXCEPT ONE.

THE 7 OF HEARTS . . .

WITH NATHAN'S NAME WRITTEN ON IT . . .

WAS STUCK TO THE CEILING.

Above his bed, peering down at him was the **7 OF HEARTS** with Nathan's name written on it. Everyone looked up, giddy, excited, transported.

I felt giddy and excited too. I said my thanks and left the room dramatically changed from the one I'd entered.

I felt changed too. But it wasn't until later that I discovered what had truly transpired, and that shifted my perspective

FOREVER.

Several months after my visit to Nathan, my wife and I were in church, and lo and behold, the visiting priest that morning was the priest I'd met that day in Nathan's hospital room.

After the service, I introduced myself. "I'm not sure if you remember me . . . my name is Jon Petz. I met you in the hospital a few months ago."

The priest immediately went from a patient kind listener of his flock to an excited, engaged, energetic person. He put his hands on my shoulders and stared at me with glistening eyes. Not saying a word, just holding me and looking into my eyes, he breathed deeper.

"We were in Nathan's room. I was the guy doing magic," I broke the uncomfortable silence.

Still without speaking, he reached into his pocket underneath his robe and brought out his wallet. He

SLOWLY OPENED IT. HE LOOKED UP AT ME AND DOWN AT THE WALLET, THEN HE REMOVED A CREDIT CARD AND HELD IT UP.

THERE IT WAS. ON THE BACK OF HIS CREDIT CARD . . . WAS THAT PICTURE OF ME.

"I KNOW EXACTLY WHO YOU ARE," THE PRIEST SAID.

"YOU HAVE NO IDEA HOW MANY PEOPLE I'VE SHARED NATHAN'S STORY WITH IN THESE PAST SEVERAL MONTHS," HE CONTINUED. "I'VE TALKED WITH FAMILIES IN PAIN NEEDING COMFORT AND I'VE ALSO BUILT A WHOLE SERVICE AROUND RECOGNIZING THE GIFTS THAT WE EACH HAVE AND MAY NOT REALIZE THEIR IMPACT."

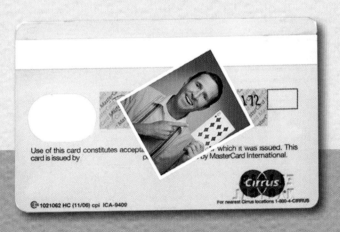

I listened intently, letting his words sink in.

What he said next went straight into my heart.

"Nathan passed away the morning after you were there."

He paused.

"And the **7 of Hearts** . . .
from the trick
you did with Nathan. . .
His family put that card . . .
in Nathan's casket
with him."

I stared at the priest, speechless.

"You see, to them, it symbolized the last happy moment they all had together as a family."

THE FLASH BACK OF THAT DAY IN NATHAN'S HOSPITAL ROOM WAS INSTANTLY UPON ME. I COULD SEE NATHAN LOOKING BRIGHT-EYED AT THE 7 OF HEARTS STUCK TO THE CEILING ABOVE HIS BED AND I COULD SEE THE SMILES ON THE FACES OF HIS FAMILY AND THE PRIEST, TOO.

NOW THE PRIEST WAS IN FRONT ME, STARING INTO MY AWESTRUCK EYES, AND SMILING KINDLY WITH HIS HAND STILL ON MY ARM. MY MOUTH PROBABLY HUNG AGAPE AS MY THOUGHTS AND EMOTIONS TANGLED TOGETHER.

A SIMPLE MOMENT VISITING A SICK CHILD AND HIS FAMILY.

It was JUST a

It was JUST a

It was JUST ...

I HAD NO IDEA THE SIGNIFICANCE OF THAT INTERACTION.

magic trick.

card trick.

a 7 of Hearts.

I WAS JUST A LOCAL MAGICIAN WHO DIDN'T EVEN WANT TO GO TO THE HOSPITAL THAT DAY.

That 7 of Hearts stuck to the ceiling, all the other cards floating down on to Nathan's bed seemed to stop now in mid-air in my memory. I felt the laughter and the lightness we all had felt in that simple moment.

His family had memorialized that beautiful moment, and they buried their precious son with that 7 of Hearts.

The priest's words rang in my ear: "We each have gifts and may not realize their impact...."

That afternoon in a little boy's hospital room had not been JUST another show.

It was a confirmation that I was indeed using my gifts and I had not fully appreciated their impact. It was also confirmation that simple moments happen around us all the time, and those are the ones that truly matter.

I share Nathan's 7 of Hearts story with audiences and here with you now to convey just that. We all have gifts. And we also have today, full of simple moments, and that too is a gift.

IT'S TIME WE RECOGNIZE AND APPRECIATE THESE GIFTS.

YOU ARE NOT "JUST"
ANYTHING.

HOW OFTEN DO YOU FALL IN
THE "JUST A" TRAP?

THAT DAMAGING PHRASE IS HEARD IN ALL ORGANIZATIONS, IN ALL SOCIAL STRUCTURES AND IN ALL LANGUAGES. WHEN WE SAY "I'M JUST A..." WHAT WE REALLY ARE UTTERING IS

"I DON'T MAKE A DIFFERENCE."

That, my friend, is not true.

I'VE SAID IT AND YOU HAVE TOO. MAYBE YOU'VE HEARD IT TODAY AT THE OFFICE, AT SCHOOL, OR AT CHURCH.

WHEN WE SAY IT, WE MINIMIZE OR BELITTLE THE IMPACT THAT WE HAVE IN:

A situation

A class

A club

Our community

Our school

Our work

Our church

A project

A meeting

Our family

Our life

You've heard it . . .
I'm "Just a"

. . . Sales Person

. . . Dad

. . . Volunteer

. . . Mom/Stay-at-home mom

. . . An Assistant

. . . Church Secretary

. . . VP of Marketing

. . . Mechanic

. . . CEO

. . . Receptionist

. . . Little League Coach

. . . Cook

. . . New Person

. . . Kid

. . . Waitress

. . . Engineer

. . . Small town girl

. . . College Student

. . . Nurse

. . . Neighbor

. . . Babysitter

. . . Student

. . . Freshman

. . . Retired Guy

. . . Driver

. . . Custodian

. . . _____

. . . _____

▲▲▲ **FILL IN YOURS** ▲▲▲

JUST A.
SO WHY DO WE SAY IT?

SOMETIMES WE LACK CONFIDENCE; PERHAPS WE DON'T LIKE OUR CURRENT JOB OR SITUATION; OFTEN WE HAVE BEEN TRAINED TO BE MODEST; WE MAY HAVE BEEN SPOKEN DOWN TO AND MADE TO FEEL THAT WAY. WE SIMPLY HAVEN'T GAINED THE PERSPECTIVE TO SEE THE IMPACT WE HAVE.

IT'S TIME **WE DO**.

IF I DIDN'T RUN INTO THE PRIEST THAT SUNDAY MORNING, WOULD THAT HAVE CHANGED THE OUTCOME OF THE STORY?

NO.

WE DON'T ALWAYS SEE THE END RESULT OF OUR INTERACTIONS. DOES THAT CHANGE THE FACT OF WHAT HAPPENED?

OF COURSE **NOT**.

YOU HAVE TOUCHED MANY PEOPLE'S LIVES AND DON'T REALIZE IT. THAT'S THE TRUTH. THAT PERSON WHO NEEDED YOUR SMILE, HUG, RECOGNITION, HELPING HAND, ENCOURAGEMENT, WORDS OF ADVICE, GUIDANCE OR LOVE, WAS IMPACTED BY YOU.

AND ON THE FLIP SIDE – HOW MANY PEOPLE HAVE AFFECTED YOUR LIFE?

HAVE YOU EVER SHARED THAT WITH THEM?

WE ARE ALL NO LONGER

JUST

ANYTHING.

YOU MAKE A DIFFERENCE. YOU HAVE GIFTS AND MAY NOT REALIZE THEIR IMPACT. IT'S TIME TO APPRECIATE ALL THAT YOU ARE. TODAY, WE ARE SHEDDING THE WORDS "JUST A" FROM OUR VOCABULARY. WE ARE REPLACING THEM WITH I AM.

"I AM" ARE THE TWO MOST POWERFUL WORDS IN OUR LANGUAGE. USE THEM TO OWN AND CELEBRATE ALL THAT YOU ARE.

I AM AN ADMINISTRATOR

I AM A SALESPERSON, A CUSTODIAN, A TAX PROFESSIONAL

I AM A HUMAN RESOURCE GENERALIST, AN ACCOUNTANT, A CUSTOMER SERVICE REP

I AM A STAY-AT-HOME DAD OR MOM

I AM A DRUMMER FOR A BAND

I AM A SPEAKER AND PERFORMER

WHAT ARE **YOU**?

I AM _____

I AM **A MAGICIAN** WHO IS NOW WRITING A BOOK TO HELP OTHERS SEE THAT THEY ARE NOT JUST ANYTHING. I AM A **SPEAKER** WHO WANTS EVERYONE TO UNDERSTAND THAT LIFE HAPPENS ALL AROUND US AND IT'S THE **SIMPLE MOMENTS** THAT HAVE THE **MOST SIGNIFICANCE**. I AM A **HUSBAND** AND **FATHER** WHO WANTS TO SHARE THESE MOMENTS WITH MY **FAMILY** AND WITH THE **WORLD**.

WHENEVER YOU FEEL THE WORDS **JUST A** RISING UP IN YOU, TAKE A BREATH. STAND UP A LITTLE TALLER. PULL YOUR SHOULDERS BACK. LIFT YOUR CHIN UP. TAKE ANOTHER DEEP BREATH.

THINK ABOUT HOW OFTEN YOU **MINIMIZE YOURSELF** EITHER BECAUSE YOU **FEEL** YOU SHOULD BE **MODEST** OR MAYBE YOU **JUST** DON'T **VALUE** YOUR OWN **GIFTS.**

L ET'S CHANGE THAT. LET'S GET YOU TO RECOGNIZE THAT YOU HAVE A SPECIAL SOMETHING TO SHARE WITH THE WORLD. SOMEONE NEEDS YOU TO SHARE IT, IN THE WAY THAT ONLY YOU CAN.

YOU ARE NOT **JUST** ANYTHING. YOU MAKE A DIFFERENCE, EVERY DAY, IN BIG WAYS AND SMALL WAYS. NEVER UNDERESTIMATE THE SMALL WAYS.

NOW ASK YOURSELF AGAIN.
WHAT ARE YOU?

I AM_____

YES, YOU ARE.

WHAT'S YOUR 7 OF HEARTS?

"I LONG TO ACCOMPLISH A GREAT AND
NOBLE TASK, BUT IT IS MY CHIEF DUTY
TO ACCOMPLISH SMALL TASKS AS IF THEY
WERE GREAT AND NOBLE."

-HELEN KELLER

Recognize
Simple
Moments

**WE ALL HAVE GIFTS.
WHAT'S YOURS?
WHAT IS YOUR 7 OF HEARTS?**

WHILE IT'S PROBABLY NOT A MAGIC TRICK, EVERY ONE OF US DOES HAVE A UNIQUE GIFT. WE ALL NEED TO EMBRACE THE CONFIDENCE TO USE OUR GIFTS, AND WE NEED TO KNOW THAT SHARING OUR GIFTS CREATES A GREATER IMPACT ON OTHERS.

YOU MAKE AN IMPACT EVERY DAY. DO YOU RECOGNIZE IT? ASK YOURSELF:

"WHAT DO I SHARE THAT IS UNIQUELY ME?" AND "WHY DO I DO WHAT I DO?"

YOUR PURPOSE MAY COME BEFORE YOUR PASSION. IT'S THE GATEWAY TO FOCUSING ON WHAT REALLY MATTERS.

NATHAN'S FAMILY BURIED HIM WITH HIS 7 OF HEARTS BECAUSE THAT WAS THE LAST TIME THEY ALL LAUGHED TOGETHER. THAT SIMPLE MOMENT WAS WHAT MATTERED. BEING TOGETHER AS A FAMILY, HAVING A SIMPLE JOY.

WITH ALL OF OUR TECHNOLOGY, WE HAVE THE OPPORTUNITY TO INTERACT AT ANYTIME WITH ANYONE, ANYWHERE IN THE WORLD. BUT ISN'T IT AMAZING HOW THE MOST MEANINGFUL CONNECTIONS ARE OFTEN THOSE THAT TAKE PLACE IN-PERSON.

DO YOU RECOGNIZE AND HONOR THOSE SIMPLE MOMENTS? IT'S THE SIMPLE MOMENTS THAT WE OFTEN TAKE FOR GRANTED. IT'S THESE THAT CAN BE THE MOST SIGNIFICANT.

Appreciate Simple Moments

DO YOU STOP AND TRULY ENGAGE IN LIFE?

WHEN WAS THE LAST TIME YOU STOPPED AND TOOK A MOMENT TO APPRECIATE THE EXPERIENCE AROUND YOU? TO LIFT YOUR HEAD UP AND REALIZE THE WONDER AND MAGIC? OR ARE YOU WATCHING LIFE THROUGH THE EYES OF SOMEONE ELSE ON SOCIAL MEDIA?

DO YOU WATCH A LIVE SHOW OR CONCERT THROUGH YOUR PHONE RECORDING THE SHOW INSTEAD OF EXPERIENCING IT FOR YOURSELF? DO YOU HAVE PERSONAL CONVERSATIONS WHILE ALSO TEXTING WITH SOMEONE ELSE?

ARE YOU TRULY LIVING, ENGAGING AND APPRECIATING WHAT LIFE HAS TO OFFER?

SOME OF THE BEST ADVICE I EVER RECEIVED CAME FROM MY BROTHER TIM THE DAY BEFORE MY WEDDING. AT A WEDDING, ALL YOUR FAMILY AND FRIENDS ARE THERE TO SEE YOU AND YET YOU HAVE ONLY A FRACTION OF TIME TO SPEAK WITH EACH OF THEM. YOU ARE PULLED IN SO MANY DIFFERENT DIRECTIONS WITH ALL THE ACTIVITIES THAT HAPPEN SO FAST.

TIM TOLD ME: "JON, TAKE A FEW MINUTES DURING THE WEDDING FESTIVITIES AND STOP. TAKE A BREAK, AND LOOK AROUND. YOU NEED TO TAKE IT ALL IN."

I DID. AND IT WAS MIRACULOUS. I SAW WHO WAS THERE. I WATCHED THEM DANCE. I WATCHED THEM LAUGH. I WATCHED THEM HUG. THESE LIFE EXPERIENCES ARE BURNED INTO MY MEMORY, NOT LANGUISHING SOMEWHERE ON A DUSTY VIDEO TAPE.

DON'T RELY ON THE PHONE OR TABLET OR INTERNET TO SHOW YOU WHAT IS GOING ON. ACTUALLY BE IN THE MOMENT AND TAKE IT ALL IN.

APPRECIATE **YOUR** SIMPLE MOMENTS.

When you can be in the moment, there is a double benefit. You reap the joy, and you also allow someone else to experience it too. We may never know the effect or exponential impact that a simple moment can have on someone else.

What if we genuinely engaged more in the possibility that simple conversations can have significant impact on another's career, family, life goals, confidence, happiness or success?

Would you engage differently if you knew that you being there mattered? Would you feel a little less fearful if you knew that the other person in your interaction needed you to show up and be you? Would you be more confident if you had a crystal ball and could see the outcome of your positive influence on the life of another?

YOU DO.

YOU ARE TOUCHING LIVES RIGHT NOW, NO MATTER WHAT YOU DO. THE VOLUNTEER MAKES A DIFFERENCE. THE TEACHER MAKES A DIFFERENCE. THE VP MAKES A DIFFERENCE. THE MAILMAN MAKES A DIFFERENCE. THE STAY-AT-HOME MOM MAKES A DIFFERENCE. THE STOCK BOY MAKES A DIFFERENCE. THE FLIGHT ATTENDANT MAKES A DIFFERENCE.

YOU MAKE A DIFFERENCE.

WHAT IF WE SHARED **OUR** UNIQUE GIFTS?

WHAT IF WE **PAUSED** AND TOOK IT ALL IN?

WHAT IF WE COULD BE IN **THE MOMENT**?

We all have an impact. Significant moments happen when you least expect and often are not aware.

That's the hardest part of this - awareness. Simple moments happen all the time. And we miss them.

As Ferris Bueller said so eloquently in the 1986 classic movie, "Life moves pretty fast. If you don't stop and look around once in a while, you could miss it."

When you pause to take it all in, you are able to realize simple moments as they are happening. These moments will be different for all of us, and can be difficult to identify in our busy lives when we have our heads down.

That's the deeper mission of the 7 of Hearts. To recognize and appreciate the simple moments. To realize there is beauty in ordinary things. There is significance in simple moments. Life will continue to move fast. It's up to us to be aware, to recognize the precious times.

I will never forget the time I almost missed it. My oldest daughter and future astronomer wanted to see her first shooting star during a meteor shower. Me? I wanted to stay in bed on this cold night.

She coaxed me to put on my coat at 3 am and soon I sat grumbling and freezing, gazing into the cloudy sky.

SEVERAL TIMES I SUGGESTED WE GO BACK INSIDE, STATING IT WAS TOO COLD AND THE CONDITIONS WERE NOT RIGHT, BUT SHE WAS COMMITTED. AND THEN IT HAPPENED. THE CLOUDS THINNED AND AN AWESOME BLAZE OF LIGHT STREAMED THROUGH THE WINTER SKY. SHE SCREAMED FOR JOY! I WAS JUST HAPPY WE COULD GO BACK TO BED.

THE FOLLOWING GROGGY MORNING, I ASKED IF SHE GOT ANY SLEEP. SHE REPLIED,

"It doesn't matter, Daddy. It was the best night of my life!"

And to think . . .

I almost missed it.

YES, I WAS THERE WITH HER, BUT I WAS GOING THROUGH THE
MOTIONS OF PARENTAL DUTY. I DIDN'T RECOGNIZE THAT THIS
SIMPLE MOMENT WAS THAT SIGNIFICANT FOR HER.

I'M GRATEFUL FOR THAT NIGHT, BECAUSE IT HAS MADE ME MORE
AWARE.

Like a shooting star, the simple moments can be easy to miss.

SIMPLE MOMENTS THAT ARE SIGNIFICANT ARE ALL AROUND US. IT'S UP TO US TO RECOGNIZE AND APPRECIATE THEM.

BE IN THE MOMENT, BIG AND SMALL. DON'T WAIT FOR "SOMEDAY." SOMEDAY IS TODAY. WE WILL NEVER HAVE MORE TIME THAN WE DO – RIGHT NOW.

When the curtain opens for your short period of time on this stage called Life, remember it is not a dress rehearsal.

It's showtime.

Deliver
Simple
Moments

SHOWTIME DOES NOT IMPLY STANDING ON A GRAND STAGE IN A SOLD-OUT VEGAS VENUE. IT'S YOUR DAILY INTERACTIONS. IT'S ABOUT TAKING IT ALL IN. IT'S ABOUT SEEING THE SIGNIFICANT IN THE SIMPLE. IT'S ABOUT INCREASING YOUR AWARENESS. IT'S BEING IN THE MOMENT.

START WITH YOUR FAMILY.

ENGAGE WITH YOUR KIDS. WALK THEM TO THE BUS STOP WHEN YOU CAN. (SOON IT WILL NOT LONGER BE COOL.) BE THE FIELD TRIP CHAPERONE. GO TO SCHOOL LUNCHTIME WHEN YOU CAN. WAIT FOR A SHOOTING STAR ON A COLD WINTER NIGHT.

WHEN YOU COME FROM WORK, BE HOME FOR THE FIRST FEW MINUTES. YES, YOU HAVE EMAIL, MAIL, TEXTS, ETC TO REPLY TO, BUT ENGAGE WITH YOUR FAMILY FIRST. IF THEY DON'T RUN UP TO YOU, THEN YOU RUN UP TO THEM FOR THAT FIRST HUG. IT NEVER BECOMES OLD, AND NOR DO YOU

LEAVE SURPRISE NOTES FOR YOUR KIDS (AND SPOUSE) IN LUNCH BOXES AND CLOSETS AND DRAWERS. IT MIGHT BE THE ONLY MEANINGFUL COMMUNICATION YOU HAVE SOME DAYS. TUCK IN YOUR KIDS AT BEDTIME. FOR SOME REASON, THIS IS WHEN THEY WILL SHARE FEELINGS, CHALLENGES AND FEARS. FOR ME, THOSE ARE THE BEST, DEEPEST, AND MOST MEANINGFUL CONVERSATIONS I HAVE EVER HAD WITH MY CHILDREN.

MAKE IT A PRIORITY TO SHARE A FEW MOMENTS WITH YOUR SPOUSE. CLEAN UP THE DISHES TOGETHER. BE ATTENTIVE AND AFFECTIONATE. BRING HOME FLOWERS JUST BECAUSE. TAKE YOUR BELOVED BY THE HAND AND GO FOR A WALK. THOSE FLEETING MOMENTS ARE THE ONES THAT ARE CHERISHED.

CREATE SIGNIFICANCE AT WORK.

WE SPEND A LOT OF TIME THERE. YOU CAN HAVE AN IMPACT, AND YOU CAN GIVE THANKS TO THOSE WHO HAVE MADE AN IMPACT ON YOU. THEY TOO MIGHT NOT REALIZE THEY HAVE GIFTS AND THAT THEIR GIFTS ARE HELPING SOMEONE.

I'VE HAD THE HONOR OF WORKING WITH COMPANIES, ASSOCIATIONS AND ORGANIZATIONS OF ALL SIZES ACROSS THE WORLD. ONE THING IS CONSISTENT. COMPANIES WHO GENUINELY APPRECIATE, RECOGNIZE AND RESPECT THEIR EMPLOYEES HAVE A MORE ENGAGED, INNOVATIVE, AND PASSIONATE WORKFORCE.

Engage with your co-workers, colleagues, team, staff and employees. Tell people why you value them. Recognize people for not only the great things, but also the everyday good things that all too often go unnoticed.

A simple heartfelt thank you goes a long way. Connect on a human to human level and remember that no one is just anything.

Increase your awareness to recognize simple moments. Create those simple moments too. Bring in treats for no reason at all. Say good morning with a smile and a look in the eye. When you ask, "How are you?" pay attention and listen to the reply.

Appreciate today.

Not Friday... not Monday.

TODAY!

REALIZE THAT WORK IS NOT THE MOST IMPORTANT RELATIONSHIP IN YOUR LIFE, BUT PEOPLE ARE.

DELIVER SIMPLE MOMENTS ANYWHERE. PRACTICE COMMON COURTESY.

HOLDING THE DOOR OPEN FOR SOMEONE CAN BE THE NICEST ACT THAT HAS HAPPENED TO THAT PERSON ALL DAY.

WAVE TO NEIGHBORS WHEN THEY DRIVE BY, EVEN IF YOU DON'T KNOW THEM. STOP FOR PEOPLE IN CROSSWALKS AND WAVE THEM THROUGH. IF SOMEONE DOES THE SAME FOR YOU, GIVE A WAVE AND NOD OF THANKS. (MY EAST COAST FRIENDS THINK I'M CRAZY.)

DONATE TIME TO YOUR COMMUNITY. WHETHER IT IS FOR A CHARITY, OR AS A VOLUNTEER AT THE ANNUAL COMMUNITY PARADE, WHEN YOU GIVE BACK YOU GET SO MUCH IN RETURN.

Little moments mean **a lot. Small gestures** can be remembered **forever.**

IF YOU REALLY WANT TO SEE HOW A SIMPLE MOMENT CAN BE SIGNIFICANT FOR SOMEONE, BRING A SMALL OUTLET SPLITTER WHEN YOU TRAVEL. ALLOW A FELLOW TRAVELER TO CHARGE THEIR PHONE WITH YOURS AT THE AIRPORT. YOU WILL MAKE THEIR DAY.

WHEN RUNNING THROUGH AN AIRPORT TO MAKE A CONNECTION, GIVE AN ENCOURAGING NOD OF "YOU CAN DO IT!" TO THE PERSON IN YOUR SAME SITUATION RUNNING THE OTHER WAY.

REMEMBER THAT ANY MOMENT CAN BE SIGNIFICANT.

REMEMBER THAT YOU HAVE A GIFT TO SHARE.

REMEMBER THAT YOU CAN MAKE SIMPLE . . . SIGNIFICANT.

BECAUSE IT'S **SHOWTIME**...
AND LIFE IS **NOT** A DRESS REHEARSAL!

THE 7 OF HEARTS MISSION

THE MISSION OF THIS BOOK IS SIMPLE. YES, I WANT IT TO REKINDLE YOUR PASSION FOR YOUR SELF-WORTH, YOUR IMPACT AND YOUR AMAZING LIFE.

THE OTHER MISSION IS TO SHARE WITH NATHAN'S FAMILY THE IMPACT THEIR CHILD IS HAVING ON THIS WORLD. I SPEAK TO ALL KINDS OF AUDIENCES AROUND THE GLOBE ABOUT CREATING SIMPLE MOMENTS OF SIGNIFICANCE AT WORK AND IN OUR LIVES. WHEN I SHARE NATHAN'S STORY, THE REACTION IS POWERFUL. PEOPLE BEGIN TO UNDERSTAND AND APPRECIATE THE MOMENTS WE ARE GIFTED EVERYDAY.

UNFORTUNATELY, I DON'T KNOW WHAT HAPPENED TO NATHAN'S FAMILY, WHERE THEY ARE, AND I DON'T EVEN KNOW THEIR LAST NAME. BUT WITH YOUR HELP, THEY WILL LEARN OF THE SIGNIFICANCE THAT NATHAN IS SHARING WITH THE WORLD.

IN THE BACK OF THIS BOOK YOU WILL FIND A 7 OF HEARTS. HERE'S MY SIMPLE REQUEST. DON'T KEEP THE CARD! GIVE IT TO SOMEONE. GIVE IT TO SOMEONE WHO HAS

MADE A DIFFERENCE IN YOUR LIFE. GIVE IT TO SOMEONE WHO IS DOING THEIR JOB, WHO IS NOT A "JUST A." GIVE IT TO SOMEONE IN A RESTAURANT, AIRPORT, SCHOOL, OR TO SOMEONE WHO PROBABLY HASN'T BEEN THANKED OR RECOGNIZED FOR MAKING A DIFFERENCE. LET THEM KNOW THEY MADE A SIMPLE MOMENT SIGNIFICANT. YOU DON'T HAVE TO TELL THEM ABOUT NATHAN, SIMPLY GIVE THEM THE CARD AND SMILE. THE CARD WILL SHARE THE STORY WITH THEM.

EACH CARD HAS A NUMBER PRINTED ON IT. PLEASE GO TO WWW.7OFHEARTS.COM AND TYPE IN YOUR NUMBER AND YOUR 7 OF HEARTS STORY. LET'S SEE IF WE CAN GET A 7 OF HEARTS TO GO AROUND THE WORLD AND SHARE THE STORIES OF HOW SIMPLE MOMENTS HAVE MADE A DIFFERENCE.

I LOVE HANDING OUT A 7 OF HEARTS WHILE TRAVELING. A FLIGHT ATTENDANT OR GATE AGENT WILL HAVE A CONFUSED LOOK WHEN I HAND THEM A CARD AND THANK THEM FOR WHAT THEY DO. AS THEY READ THE BACK OF THE CARD, A WONDERFUL SMILE REPLACES THE CONFUSION ON THEIR FACE.

I ALSO LOVE TO READ AND SHARE THE STORIES THAT PEOPLE POST ON THE WEBSITE AS THESE CARDS MOVE FROM HAND TO HAND.

THE FIRST TIME I EXPERIENCED A 7 OF HEARTS STORY IN THE FLESH, IT WAS MAGICAL. I HAD DELIVERED A KEYNOTE ADDRESS THAT INCLUDED NATHAN'S STORY AND HAD GIVEN EVERYONE IN THE audience a 7 of Hearts. A woman excitedly approached me.

She exclaimed, "I have a 7 of Hearts!"

"Yes, everyone received one. Would you like another?" I looked at her slightly puzzled.

"No," she said. "You don't understand. I got one months ago! One like this! Someone gave me one of your 7 of Hearts! It's tacked on my bulletin board in my cube."

My eyes widened and my eyebrows went up.

She continued, "My boss gave it to me for an event I was working on. I was "just" doing my job and he thanked me for my impact! It felt so good to get that compliment. I put the 7 of Hearts up on my board to remind me that I do make a difference!"

That was when I knew the 7 of Hearts mission was taking effect. I gave her a hug, and I admit I had a tear in my eye.

The words of the priest rang in my ear. "We all have gifts...." I smiled as I remembered Nathan and his family squealing with laughter that last day they had together.

The ultimate goal is that one day, somehow, somewhere, somebody is going to pass that card to someone in Nathan's family. They too will recognize the impact they have made on the world.

GO AHEAD, TAKE THE CARD NOW. PUT IT IN YOUR WALLET OR PURSE, AND GIVE IT TO THE RIGHT PERSON AT THE RIGHT TIME, SOMEONE WHO MADE A SIMPLE MOMENT SPECIAL FOR YOU.

IF YOU NEED MORE CARDS,
PLEASE VISIT WWW.7OFHEARTS.COM.

TOGETHER WE CAN ACCOMPLISH GREAT THINGS. TOGETHER OUR IMPACT IS TRULY MAGICAL.

MIRACLES & MAGIC™

A Magical Adventure

Saturday, April 27th 2002 Featuring the Magic and Illusion of Jonathan Petz

POSTER FROM OUR FIRST SHOW IN 2002.
FEATURING: LAUREN COLBY (1988-2007)

A LOT HAS HAPPENED SINCE THAT DAY IN THE HOSPITAL. FOLLOWING THAT EXPERIENCE, MY WIFE AND I DECIDED, "IT'S SHOWTIME." WE PUT TOGETHER A COMEDY-MAGIC AND ILLUSION SHOW TO BENEFIT THESE AMAZING KIDS AND THEIR FAMILIES WHO ARE FIGHTING LIFE THREATENING ILLNESSES.

OUR MISSION? TO GIVE SICK KIDS AND THEIR FAMILIES A CHANCE TO FORGET ABOUT SHOTS, CHEMO, AND HOSPITAL BEDS FOR A FEW HOURS AND COME EXPERIENCE THE LAUGHTER, JOY AND WONDERMENT OF MAGIC.

WE SOLD TICKETS OUT OF OUR KITCHEN AND HOSTED THE SHOW AT A LOCAL HIGH SCHOOL THEATER. WE INITIALLY PARTNERED WITH THE "A KID AGAIN" ORGANIZATION TO MAKE IT A REALITY. A KID AGAIN'S MISSION IS TO FOSTER HOPE, HAPPINESS, AND HEALING FOR FAMILIES RAISING KIDS WITH LIFE THREATENING ILLNESSES (WWW.AKIDAGAIN.ORG)

KYLE NOBLE HOLDING HIS MAGIC WAND (1998-2006)

OUR FIRST YEAR WE RAISED ABOUT $5000 AND WERE ABLE TO SHARE MAGIC WITH HUNDREDS OF KIDS WHO NEEDED IT MOST.

SINCE THAT FIRST YEAR, WE GREW THE SHOW, MOVED TO A PRIME TIME THEATER AND EXPANDED TO THREE CITIES. WE'VE HAD THE BEST MAGICIANS IN THE WORLD JOIN IN THE MISSION AND SHARE THEIR TALENTS AND WONDER WITH BRIGHT-EYED ADULTS AND CHILDREN ALIKE. OUR MIRACLES & MAGIC™ SHOW HAS NOW GROSSED NEARLY $1,500,000 FOR CHARITY AND HAS SHARED LAUGHTER AND JOY WITH THOUSANDS OF FAMILIES.

ALL THIS STEMMED FROM A SIMPLE CARD TRICK . . .

A 7 OF HEARTS. . .
A WIDE-EYED NATHAN . . .
AND A FEW WORDS
WITH A PRIEST.

ONE SIMPLE TRICK THAT HAD SUCH SIGNIFICANCE FOR NATHAN'S FAMILY, AND IN MY LIFE, AND FOR WHICH I NOW FEEL COMPELLED TO SHARE WITH OTHERS.

MY HOPE IS TO RAISE $10,000,000 AND BEYOND TO HELP THESE KIDS. THANK YOU FOR YOUR PURCHASE OF THIS BOOK AS PROCEEDS GO TO THIS MISSION.

TO LEARN MORE, TO CONTRIBUTE, OR TO GET INVOLVED, PLEASE VISIT WWW.7OFHEARTS.COM OR WWW.MIRACLESANDMAGIC.COM

THANK YOU FOR YOUR IMPACT.

THANK YOU FOR SHARING A SIMPLE MOMENT AND MAKING IT SIGNIFICANT SIMPLY BY READING THIS BOOK.

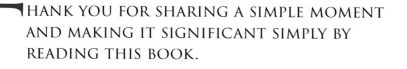

REMEMBER THAT YOU ARE NOT **JUST** ANYTHING. **YOU** MAKE A DIFFERENCE.

RECOGNIZE THE OPPORTUNITY TO MAKE A SIMPLE MOMENT . . . SIGNIFICANT.

APPRECIATE **YOUR** SIMPLE MOMENTS AND TAKE THEM ALL IN.

DELIVER SIMPLE MOMENTS BY SHARING YOUR GIFT WITH THE WORLD.

YOU WILL **NEVER** HAVE MORE TIME THAT YOU DO RIGHT NOW.

"And BABY . . .

IT'S SHOWTIME

– and Life is not a dress rehearsal."

- Jon Petz

Gabriel Taylor
(2005 – 2011)

ABOUT THE AUTHOR:

Jon Petz is the founder of **Bore No More**. He and his company work with organizations that want to create an atmosphere of energy and engagement to empower high performing teams and individuals.

Jon brings this passion and energy for performance to stages across the world as an in-demand speaker at corporate and association events. He draws on his diverse experience as a corporate executive, social experimenter, event emcee and comedy magician. Jon speaks on a variety of topics, including personal performance and impact, customer experience and passion, mixed with the energy and entertainment that is uniquely and unequivocally Jon Petz.

USA Today, The Wall Street Journal, CNBC, ABC News, Success Magazine and many other media outlets have covered the success of Jon Petz as an author, thought leader and engagement expert. His most recent book, *Boring Meetings Suck™,* (Wiley 2011) was listed in *Inc. Magazine* as a top ten Business book.

Jon is also the founder of *Miracles & Magic™*. A Las Vegas style grand illusion and comedy magic show that provides children with life threatening illnesses a chance to forget about the treatments, shots and hospital, and instead shares the wonder and joy of comedy magic and illusion. This very book is the story of how that event came to be.

Jon lives in Columbus, Ohio with his family at *"Camp Petz"* (as they affectionately call it).

Jon has authored or co-authored:

Boring Meeting Suck
Best of the Best
Unlocking The Secrets

To check availability for an event, or for more information on Jon as a speaker please contact the **Bore No More** office at **877-457-3981**.

www.JonPetz.com

www.BoringMeetingsSuck.com

www.7ofHearts.com

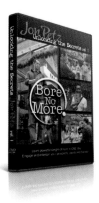